# FIESTA!

# ARGENTINA

## GROLIER

An Imprint of Scholastic Library Publishing
Danbury, Connecticut

Published for Grolier,
an imprint of Scholastic Library Publishing
Old Sherman Turnpike, Danbury, Connecticut 06816
by Times Editions,
an imprint of Times Media Pte Ltd

Copyright © 2004 Times Media Pte Ltd, Singapore
First Grolier Printing 2004

Set ISBN: 0-7172-5788-6
Volume ISBN: 0-7172-5789-4

**Library of Congress Cataloging-in-Publication Data**
Argentina.
p. cm.—(Fiesta!)
Summary: Discusses the festivals and holidays of Argentina and how the songs, food,
and traditions associated with these celebrations reflect the culture of the people.
1. Festivals—Argentina—Juvenile literature. 2. Argentina—Social life and customs—Juvenile literature.
[1. Festivals—Argentina. 2. Holidays—Argentina. 3. Argentina—Social life and customs.]
I. Grolier (Firm). II. Fiesta! (Danbury, Conn.)
GT4831.A2A74  2004
394.2682—dc21          2003044838

*For this volume*
Author: Tan Mae Lynn
Editor: Yeo Puay Khoon
Designer: Geoslyn Lim
Production: Nor Sidah Haron
Crafts and Recipes produced by Stephen Russell

Printed in Malaysia

Adult supervision advised for all crafts and recipes,
particularly those involving sharp instruments and heat.

# CONTENTS

# ARGENTINA

*The second largest country in South America, República Argentina gained independence from Spain in 1816. It has a population of about 37 million people, 85 percent of whom are of European descent. The others are made up of indigenous people — native Indian groups.*

▼ **Buenos Aires** is the capital of Argentina. A cosmopolitan city, it is also the most populated province in the country. Buenos Aires is the country's center of cultural and economic activity. One of the oldest buildings in Buenos Aires, the Cabildo at Plaza de Mayo, used to be the colonial town hall during Spanish rule. Now it has been turned into a museum.

▲ **The Virgin of Luján** is the patron saint of Argentina. Every year, thousands of people travel to a small city west of Buenos Aires where the virgin's statue resides to pray to her.

BOLIVIA

Humahuaca

Tilcara

CHILE

PARAGUAY

BRAZIL

Salta

Tucumán

Resistencia

Corrientes

Córdoba

San Juan

Santa Fe

PACIFIC
OCEAN

Paraná

Rosario

URUGUAY

Mendoza

BUENOS AIRES

La Plata

Mar del Plata

Bahía Blanca

ATLANTIC
OCEAN

FALKLAND
ISLANDS

▲ **Eva Duarte Perón** was an actress. She became the second wife of Juan Perón and used her popularity and position to establish various movements for women and the poor. Her ability to touch the lives of the masses gave her a saintly presence among Argentineans. The Eva Perón fascination still continues now, many years after her death.

▶ **Soccer** is an Argentine obsession. The most popular player in Argentina's soccer history is Diego Maradona who has since become a national icon.

5

# RELIGIONS

*Most Argentineans are Catholic. Many of the country's
holidays and festivals are related to the religion, with many
commemorating the day by going to church for mass.*

*The indigenous people of Argentina
produced beautifully crafted ceramic
animal figurines.*

THE MAJORITY OF Argentineans
are of European descent, in particular
of Italian and Spanish origins.
Furthermore, with the influence of
its earlier Spanish colonizers prior
to 1816 Catholicism has gained a
strong foothold in the lives of
Argentineans.

Although about 90 percent of the
population claims to be Catholic, only
about 20 percent go to church regularly.
However, children are usually given
biblical names or saints' names according
to the Spanish language. On religious
holidays and feast days thousands
flock to churches to participate in
the festivities.

There are also other Christian
groups in Argentina today. They
include Protestants and Armenian
and Orthodox Christians. Argentina
also has the largest Jewish population in
Latin America. Most of them came from
Europe between the late nineteenth and
early twentieth centuries and live
mostly in Buenos Aires.

Many indigenous people
continue to practice their
traditional beliefs. Native Indian
religions often reflect the people's
strong connections with nature.
Some indigenous communities,
like the Mestizo and Colla people,
have blended Catholic beliefs and
practices with their traditional
forms of worship and practice.

Popular beliefs that diverge from official doctrine are also common. Spiritualism and worship of the dead are also a part of Argentine society. Many people make pilgrimages to the resting places of the dead, especially of famous people like Eva Perón.

*This Catholic decorative piece depicts the Virgin Mary carrying a young Jesus Christ.*

# GREETINGS FROM **ARGENTINA!**

The official language of Argentina is Spanish. Argentinean Spanish is slightly different from the Spanish spoken in Spain. It can sometimes sound more Italian than Spanish. Many other languages are also spoken in Argentina. They include Italian, German, English, and French. Some of the indigenous languages that are still alive today are Tehuelche, Guarani, and Quechua. The colonization of Argentina by the Spaniards is largely responsible for the dominance of the Spanish language today. However, Italian is also widely understood since Italians made up the largest immigrant group from Europe during the early twentieth century.

In the late nineteenth century a slang called *lunfardo* originated in the slums of Buenos Aires. It has elements of Spanish, Italian, Portuguese, and some other languages. A common way of creating words in the slang was to reverse syllables. For example, in *lunfardo* the word "tango" is "gotan." Most Argentineans today are familiar with only a few words of *lunfardo*.

## How do you say...

Hello!
**Hola!**

Goodbye!
**Adiós!**

Thank you
**Gracias**

Peace
**Paz**

Please
**Por favor**

I'm sorry
**Lo siento**

# NAVIDAD

**Since Argentina is a mainly Catholic country, Christmas is a major festival. It is celebrated on December 25 in honor of the birth of Jesus Christ.**

In Argentina Christmas celebrations are similar to those of other western nations. At the start of Advent families put up Christmas trees at home and have fun decorating them with ornaments, lights, and cotton to imitate snow. Houses are filled with decorations to reflect festivities. Christmas garlands are made, and the Nativity scene, with the manger where Christ was born, is put together at home.

Christmas is mostly a family-oriented occasion. On Christmas Eve many people attend midnight mass before enjoying a late dinner together. Others go to church on Christmas day before gathering for a big meal.

Because of the lovely

## NINOS ENVUETTAS

A popular Christmas dish in Argentina is ninos envuettas. Like most Argentine dishes, it contains a lot of beef.

### SERVES 4

*4 slices of beef steak*
*8 oz minced meat*
*1/2 medium onion, chopped*
*2 hard-boiled eggs*
*Spices*

**1** Ask an adult to cut the beef into strips of about 3 inches length.

**2** Slice the hard-boiled eggs.

**3** Mix the minced meat, onions, and eggs in a bowl. Add spices, and mix.

**4** Using a spoon, put some minced meat mix on each beef strip. Wrap each strip with the stuffing into a small roll.

**5** Place rolls on a pan, and bake in oven until brown and tender.

*Traditionally, champagne is used for toasts after dinner on Christmas Eve.*

weather lots of people celebrate with either a picnic or barbecue. Dinner is made up of holiday food such as roast pork, turkey, stuffed tomatoes, and meat pies. Cake is served after dinner with a customary toast with champagne.

Christmas rituals such as giving presents, banquets, champagne, cakes, and fireworks at midnight are also followed.

Carolers visit homes, singing and spreading Christmas cheer. Families gather to sing or to watch the fireworks at midnight. In recent times gifts are exchanged on Christmas day or on the eve at the stroke of midnight.

A unique Christmas practice in Argentina can be seen on the eve of Epiphany. On January 5 children put their shoes under the Christmas tree or beside their beds. They also leave hay and water outside their house for the horses of the Three Wise Men, or Magi. It is believed that the Magi bring Christmas gifts to children who leave out the hay and water. The hay and water are to provide them with a meal for their tiring journey to Bethlehem.

*Christmas trees are decorated with cotton to imitate snowfall during Christmas.*

# MAKE A CHRISTMAS SNOW GLOBE

## YOU WILL NEED

*Small glass jar with lid*
*Hot-glue gun*
*Sand (optional)*
*Baby oil*
*Egg shells or glitter*
*Rolling pin*
*Plastic zip-lock bag*
*Plastic ornament*
 *(e.g., miniature nativity scene,*
 *an angel, or Santa Claus)*
*Small piece of cloth (optional)*
*Rubber band (optional)*
*Ribbon (optional)*

**1** Wash the empty jar, and dry it completely. There should be no water droplets in the jar.

**2** Ask an adult to plug in the hot-glue gun to warm it up.

**3** Put the jar lid upside down on a table, and stand your plastic ornament in the center of the lid. Make sure that the ornament fits into the jar, and that the jar can be closed.

**4** Ask an adult to help you stick the ornament onto the lid with hot glue.

**5** If too much glue is showing, you can cover it up with sand.

**10** If you want, you can cut out a piece of cloth just a little bigger than the size of the lid and wrap it around the lid with a rubber band. Tie a ribbon around the lid to hide the rubber band.

**6** Put the egg shells into a large zip-lock bag. Remember to leave a narrow gap and not to seal it completely. Using a rolling pin, crush the shells into small pieces.

**7** After the glue has cooled, pour baby oil into the jar until it is full.

**8** Add as many crushed egg shells ("snow") to the jar as you like. If you want your snow to sparkle, add some glitter as well.

**9** Get an adult to help you put hot glue on the outside edge of the jar's lid, then carefully screw the lid on as tightly as possible so that the oil doesn't run out.

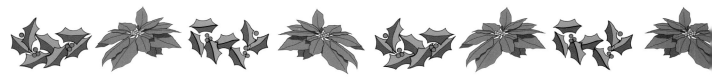

# LEYENDA DEL FLORES DE NOCHE BUENA

*The poinsettia is a popular flower for Christmas time in many countries.*

*The legend of the poinsettia comes from Mexico.*

MARIA AND HER LITTLE brother Pablo looked forward to Christmas every year. During this festive season a large manger scene where Jesus Christ was born would be set up in the village church. Parades would fill the streets on the days leading up to Christmas.

Maria and Pablo loved Christmas, but were very poor and always felt sad because they could not afford to buy presents. They wished they could get a gift to bring to church for Baby Jesus.

Nevertheless, on one Christmas Eve the two children went to church to attend mass. Everyone held gifts in their hands and presented them to Baby Jesus. Maria and Pablo were hesitant to approach the manger scene. Then Pablo said to his sister: "I am sure that even the most humble gift, if given in love, will be acceptable in His eyes."

Not knowing what else to do, Maria and her brother Pablo knelt by the side of the road and gathered a handful of weeds. They carefully made them into a small bouquet and decided

to take it as their gift to Baby Jesus. Other children teased them. They looked at their gift and felt sad because of the humbleness of their offering. Maria and Pablo did not say anything since it was the best thing they could offer, and they put their bouquet of weeds and leaves around the manger.

Suddenly the green leaves turned into bright red petals. Soon the manger was filled with beautiful star-shaped flowers. All those who saw the change were certain they had witnessed a Christmas miracle. And from that day on, the flowers were known as *Flores de Noche Buena,* or Flowers of the Holy Night.

# DÍA DE LA INDEPENDENCIA

*Military men dress up in their best attire for the July 9 military parade, even putting on their guns at their sides.*

**Argentina celebrates two national liberation days in a year, one on May 25 and another on July 9.**

On May 25 Argentineans remember the May Revolution of 1810. On that day resistance movements were in place against their Spanish colonizers. When British troops attacked Buenos Aires, the townspeople revolted, drove them out, and formed a whole new government under the *Provincias Unidas del Río de la Plata*, or the United Provinces of the Río de la Plata. It was governed on behalf of King Fernando VII, who was being held captive by Napoleon. It was not until July 9, 1816, that representatives from various provinces gathered at Tucumán for a congressional meeting that officially declared the independence of the *Provincias Unidas de América del Sur*, or United Provinces of South America.

During the May 25 Independence Day lavish parades are held, with military officers marching through the town plaza and *gauchos* riding on horseback. People dress up in costumes and masks of the nineteenth century, and there is

a reenactment of the revolutionary struggle and the Declaration of Independence.

On July 9 an early mass is celebrated to mark the official day of independence. Franciscan priests hang garlands, lanterns, and flags on the doors of churches. There are also parades in which military men dress up in formal attire complete with sabers and guns, while people go out on the streets to feast and celebrate. At the city square people stay up and dance till the early hours of the morning.

*Gauchos on horses ride all the way through the town plaza as part of the parade.*

*Argentinean flags are hung up everywhere on buildings and along streets to celebrate the country's independence.*

# FIESTA DE LA VENDIMIA

*This annual event takes place in the wine-producing province of Mendoza on the first Saturday of March and lasts for a week. The wine harvest festival is a celebration of reaping the fruits from the land.*

*Grapes are used to make wine for mass and are a good source of nutrition as well.*

The Fiesta de la Vendimia Wine Festival attracts people from all around the world. It boosts the local economy and marks the harvesting of grapes by celebrating the end of the work in the vineyards.

The festival recognizes the ancestors of people living in Mendoza and is to thank those who have made the province a better place. Vendimia is an important time for the city of Mendoza because 70 percent of Argentinean wine is produced here.

Vendimia originated in the colonial times. The grapevines were often linked with spiritual work because wine was needed to celebrate mass. An orchard was planted next to the chapels to make the wine served at mass.

*Mules, together with horses, gauchos, and wagons are paraded down the street because they represent the rural way of life.*

The festival celebrates the end of the farmers' work on the land, and the fruits received are the prize for their efforts. The main attractions of the week-long celebrations are the Blessing of the Fruit, White Way of the Queens, and a beauty pageant.

During the festival week the archbishop of Mendoza blesses the grapes and wine. The ceremony is an act of gratitude to God for the fruits received and honors

# CANTO A MENDOZA

Men - do - za,

tierra del sol y del bu - en vi - no...

Men-do - za,

la de los An-des in - fi - ni - tos...

Mi tier - ra,

la de las ca - lles men - do - ci - nas...

Men - do - za,

la que acu - nó la li - ber - tad!

Mendoza,
ground of the sun and of the
good wine...
Mendoza,
of the infinite Andes...
My land,
of the Mendozan streets...
Mendoza,
the one that cradles liberty!

the Virgin of the Carodilla. An image of the virgin was brought to the town, and a chapel was built for her. People pray to her to look after the welfare of the town and its livelihood — the grapevines.

*Carrusel* is a party and a parade of gauchos, horses, wagons, and mules as symbols of rural life. Every year the *Canto a Mendoza*, or Song to Mendoza, is performed to entertain the locals and tourists.

Celebrations end with a spectacular display of fireworks.

*The prettiest woman in the pageant is crowned as the Wine Harvest Queen at the end of the festival.*

# CARNAVAL

*Most cities run their own carnival parades and parties, but the most popular and enthusiastic parties are mainly in the northern provinces. Carnivals in different cities tend to vary because of different traditions.*

*Everyone throws water balloons at each other during Carnaval, and no one is spared, not even the old and well-dressed.*

The Carnaval is the most popular party in the whole of South America. Carnaval, or Carnival, is an event that comes from pagan-Catholic practices.

Business comes to a halt during Carnaval as people dressed in fancy costumes throng all the streets to dance and sing. Festivities usually begin on the weekend before Ash Wednesday in late February. Just like most other major parties and celebrations in the country, the carnival lasts for almost a week. People dress up in elaborate costumes and take part in processions along the street. Water balloons are thrown at anyone and everyone in sight.

In the northeastern parts of the country celebrations are mixed with the customs of the native people. Corn beer, or *chicha*, is very popular with revelers in Humahuaca, and so is the music of the Quecha Indians. In the city of Corrientes

festivities are strongly influenced by European traditions.

The party in Tilcara is popular with artists, and there are lots of flowers and parades everywhere. To celebrate, villagers light firecrackers to provoke the devil. Boys dress up as devils and toss a devil-figure around the other happy revelers. Together with a band, they lead a procession and dance through the streets until it reaches the town hall. The music and dancing carry on until the early hours of the morning.

The more religious sides of the party in Tilcara are the flowered statues and the floral arrangements representing the Stations of the Cross that are displayed along the streets.

*People wear fancy masks and dress up in colorful costumes for the procession down the streets.*

*Chicha is a beer made from fermented corn and water. Festival-goers drink a lot of it during the Carnaval celebrations.*

19

# LA PASCUA

*Easter is both a joyful and a somber time for people since it marks the death of Jesus Christ and his resurrection to the Kingdom of God.*

Easter, or *la Pascua*, celebrations begin on Palm Sunday in Argentina. Holy Week, or *Semana Santa*, is the most important religious festival for most of Latin America.

Festivities and customs relating to Easter tend to be more elaborate and dramatic in Latin America than western countries. Throughout Holy Week there are religious rituals and street processions taking place. Often, in many cities people reenact Jesus Christ's last supper, his betrayal, and judgment.

*During La Pascua nicely wrapped chocolate eggs are given to children as gifts.*

Participants dress in costumes and carry large wooden crosses to act out the Stations of the Cross, Jesus's crucifixion, and his final resurrection. The participants and even observers can sometimes get very emotional during these displays.

During this time of year many Catholics can be seen paying homage, attending mass, and also participating in religious observations.

*This decorative dish depicts Jesus Christ and his twelve disciples at the Last Supper.*

# CRISTO HA RESUCITADO

Christ has returned to life: Alleluia!
Joyfully hear the singing today: Alleluia!
With trumpets proclaim: Alleluia!
Heaven and Earth, make the sound: Alleluia!

# MAKE A BURNED MATCH CROSS

### YOU WILL NEED
*Burned matches (only the tip of the match should be burned)*
*Cardboard*
*Glue*

**1** On a rectangular piece of cardboard, draw a vertical line down the center. Then draw a horizontal line about $1/_3$ the way down from the top of the cardboard.

**2** Cut off the tips of two matchsticks. Cut one of them in half. Glue each half onto each side of the vertical line.

**3** Cut the other matchstick into quarters. Glue the two quarters onto the horizontal line.

NB: Do not attempt to burn the matches on your own.
Ask an adult for help.

**4** Beginning with one right-angle corner of the cross, glue the matchsticks on at approximately 45 degree angles. Stick the first matchstick directly where the first two guide sticks cross.

**5** Stick two matchsticks on either side of the first, lining them up parallel to the first matchstick and against the vertical and horizontal guides.

**6** Continue adding matchsticks for the slanted parts until all four sides are done.

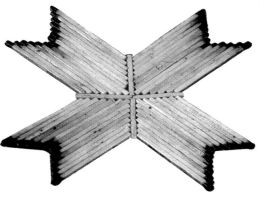

**7** When all four slanted sides are completed, add the vertical and horizontal pieces. The bottom of the matches should touch the matches in the slanted blocks.

**8** Add an additional vertical row of matches at the bottom of the cross.

# WORLD TANGO FESTIVAL

**The sensual music and dance popularly known as the tango has its roots in Argentina.**

*Men wear hats when they dance the tango.*

Born in the slums of the city of Buenos Aires in the mid-nineteenth century, tango was created by European immigrants, local peasants from inland, and some disadvantaged *porteño*, or people born in the capital, who gathered to share their cultures and to form a new social class. This group of people began to create new cultural expressions from their interaction, perhaps as a way of creating a group identity for themselves. This was the beginning of tango.

Because the dance originated from the lower classes, it was shunned by the conservative upper-class people, particularly since it gained popularity in saloons during the late 1800s. Today the great popularity of tango has broken class barriers

*Tango shoes usually have a glittery appearance on top and a smooth sole on the bottom to help dancers easily slide across the wooden floor.*

and has even spread to many European countries.

So, it is only right that the World Tango Festival is held in Buenos Aires. During the month of October tango fans from all over the world descend onto the capital for a week-long fiesta. Visitors can enjoy shows by famous tango dancers and musicians, take dance classes from professionals, and even compete in an International Tango Dance Tournament. The party goes on for seven days and seven nights, and all the participants and visitors get to enjoy endless tango fun.

During the festival tours are also given for visitors to go to tango landmarks in the city, as well as the traditional Buenos Aires tango party place, or *Milonga*.

*Argentinean women like to dress up in their best when dancing the tango.*

# Día de la Tradición

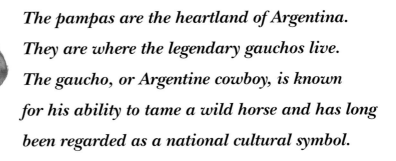

**The pampas are the heartland of Argentina. They are where the legendary gauchos live. The gaucho, or Argentine cowboy, is known for his ability to tame a wild horse and has long been regarded as a national cultural symbol.**

*Gauchos are skillful at rounding up animals such as bulls, cows, and oxen.*

In November every year many ranch areas on the vast grasslands of the pampas – about 360 miles south of Buenos Aires – celebrate *Día de la Tradición*, or Day of the Gaucho. The festival honors the gaucho as the perfect example of Argentinean men and culture. He has a rough, tough image and is also a great horseman.

Traditionally gauchos tamed wild horses, herded cattle, and were known for their resilience and courage. Their skills were crucial to early settlers who needed help in tending to their cattle herds. This annual festival highlights the life of a gaucho with dancing, singing, horse parades, and eating the best meat.

These Argentinean cowboys are less well known for their singing and dancing. However, gauchos have passed on the melancholic song *milonga* and the *pavada* dance until today. The latter is a fast and furious dance with fancy steps. Rival gauchos dance the *pavada* and try to better one another with their footwork. It is said

*Every gaucho carries a chucillo, both as a weapon and as an all-purpose tool.*

that both the *milonga* and the *pavada* influenced the birth of tango.

Gauchos like to drink a tea called *yerba maté*. It is made from the leaves of the South American holly plant and is usually shared by a group of gauchos. The *yerba maté* is brewed in a gourd-shaped container called a *maté* with warm but not boiling water. Then it is sipped with a thin tube called a *bombilla*. The *maté* is passed around in a circle from one gaucho to the next. The same drink is shared by every man as a symbol of their friendship.

*The scarf can be worn in different ways, either around the neck as an ornament or over the head to protect the gaucho from the weather.*

# CHIMICHURRI

This is a very popular sauce commonly used with beef or added to barbecued meat.

1 Put all the ingredients into a jar with a tight-fitting lid.

2 Use a spoon to stir and mix the ingredients thoroughly.

3 Screw the jar's lid on tightly, and let it stand for a minimum of two hours.

4 The sauce can be used to marinate meat two hours before barbequing or cooking.

5 Using a brush, put some of the sauce on bread. Toast the bread to make spicy garlic bread.

## YOU WILL NEED
*4 oz olive oil*
*4 oz white wine vinegar*
*1 onion, chopped*
*2 garlic cloves, pressed*
*2 thsp parsley, chopped*
*1 tsp dried oregano*
*1 tsp cayenne pepper*
*1 tbsp lemon juice*
*Salt to taste*

# THE YERBA MATÉ

*Sometimes in the Paraguayan maté fields people would see a beautiful blonde girl whose eyes reflected the innocence and honesty of her soul. She is the spirit of yerba maté.*

YARÍ, THE MOON GODDESS, looked down at Earth, which was covered with forests. The more she gazed at the Earth, the more she yearned for a closer look.

One day Yarí called on Araí, the pink cloud of dust, to accompany her down to Earth. The two of them turned into two beautiful ladies. They were walking along in the woods and were starting to feel tired. They saw a cottage in the distance and walked toward it in the hope of getting some rest there.

Suddenly they heard a noise. A jaguar leaped at them, but an arrow brought the animal down. Then a second arrow went through its heart.

An old man had come to their rescue. He invited them back to the hut where he lived with his wife and daughter. At home the family treated them with warmth and kindness. They explained that Tupá, the powerful god of the Guaranies, frowns on those who are not welcoming to their guests. The old man told Yarí and Araí that he had decided to move far away from the community so that his daughter could preserve the virtues that Tupá had bestowed on her.

The next day, Yarí and Araí decided to leave. The man's wife and daughter bid them farewell, and the man escorted them out. When Yarí and Araí were alone, they lost their human shapes and returned to heaven to look for a gift for the family.

One night Yarí and Araí put the family into deep sleep. While they slept soundly, Yarí sowed light blue seeds in front of their hut, and Araí poured sweet and soft rain to wet the ground.

When morning came, there were short trees with dark-green leaves and white flowers in front of the hut. The man woke up and was about to set out into the forest when he saw the trees

outside. He was shocked. He quickly called for his wife and daughter. As the family marveled at the sight, they fell on their knees onto the wet ground.

Just then Yarí appeared before them in the shape of the woman they had met earlier. She said: "I am Yarí, the moon goddess. I want to reward you for your goodness. This new plant is the *yerba maté*. From now on it will be the symbol of friendship for you and for all men of this region. Your daughter will live forever, and she will never lose the goodness and innocence of her heart. She will be the spirit of *yerba maté*."

Having said that, the goddess got them to their feet and taught them how to toast and drink the *maté*.

Years later the old couple passed away. Their daughter, after fulfilling her duties, disappeared from Earth. From that day onward people sometimes see a girl with blonde hair standing in the *yerba maté* fields looking over the plant.

# FESTIVAL DE COSQUÍN

***In the province of Córdoba lies the city of Cosquín, the national capital of folklore. Over the last forty years the city has gained a reputation for its annual music and arts festival – the National Festival of Folklore.***

*Aspiring musicians such as guitar players attend the National Festival of Folklore to perform folk songs.*

The festival takes place during the last two weeks of January. It was first held in 1961 as an effort to promote the city's tourism and to stimulate the local economy. Over the years the festival has grown so big that it attracts people from all over Argentina as well as around the world.

People come to discover the true spirit of Cosquín and Argentina, and to enjoy the festivities that reflect a merging of cultural and popular roots.

Argentina's famous artists gather in Cosquín to perform and share their art. It is also an important event for young musicians and artists to showcase their work. Here everyone gets to enjoy the different shades of national folklore through poetry, song, music, and even dance.

Later the National Art and Crafts Fair was also included as part of this festival. People not only gathered to enjoy music but also to enjoy various art exhibitions.

Today the National Festival of Folklore has become more than just a showcase of talent. Delegations of musicians and artists, particularly from South America, meet during this annual event. It is seen as an important occasion that fosters good will and builds friendship.

*Empanadas, or turnovers, are made of ground beef filling wrapped in dough. They are served either fried or baked and are eaten during popular festivals.*

# WORDS TO KNOW

**Advent:** The season including the four Sundays before Christmas.

**Customary:** Based on tradition.

**Epiphany:** The moment when Jesus Christ appeared to the Three Wise Men.

**Folklore:** Traditional beliefs, stories, or customs passed down through word of mouth over generations.

**Gaucho:** An Argentinean cowboy.

**Magi:** The Three Wise Men who brought gifts to the infant Jesus.

**Mass:** A religious service that is held in a Roman Catholic church.

**Melancholic:** Something that makes you sad.

**Mendocino:** A native of Mendoza.

**Mestizo:** A person of mixed racial ancestry, especially of mixed European and Native American ancestry.

**Native Indians:** The indigenous people of the Americas.

**Patron saint:** A saint who protects and guides a person, people, state, or nation.

**Resurrection:** The rising of Jesus Christ into Heaven.

**Revolution:** The overthrowing of a current system of government by force.

**Rituals:** Religious or solemn ceremonies performed in a set order.

**Saber:** A heavy sword with a slightly curved blade.

**Stations of the Cross:** Represent the stages at which Jesus was condemned to die until he was laid down to rest in the tomb.

---

## ACKNOWLEDGMENTS

WITH THANKS TO:
Las Pampas El Restaurante y la Barra, Singapore, Daphne Rodrigues, Krisinder Mukhtiar Kaur, Nafisah Ismail, Joseph Frois, and Senthamarai Rogawansamy for the loan of artifacts.

PHOTOGRAPHS BY:
Haga Library, Japan (cover), Eduardo Gil (p. 6 left, p. 26 bottom), Sam Yeo (p. 6 right, p. 7, p. 14 left, p. 15 bottom, p. 24 bottom, p. 25, p. 26 top, p. 27 top, p. 30 bottom), Yu Hui Ying (all other pictures).

ILLUSTRATIONS BY:
Enrico Sallustio (p.1, pp. 4-5, p. 7, p. 24, p. 29). Lee Kowling (p. 13).

31

# SET CONTENTS